CHOSEN TO RATTLE

CHOSEN TO RATTLE

A Story About David Wiggins
A Hometown Hero

SUE JARRIEL GARCIA

AuthorHouse™ LLC
1663 Liberty Drive
Bloomington, IN 47403
www.authorhouse.com
Phone: 1-800-839-8640

Published by AuthorHouse 02/20/2014

ISBN: 978-1-4918-6637-5 (sc)
ISBN: 978-1-4918-6638-2 (hc)
ISBN: 978-1-4918-6639-9 (e)

Library of Congress Control Number: 2014903243

CONTENTS

DEDICATION

I would like to dedicate this book to my loving family. They have been a great inspiration to me and my endeavors to become an author. To my husband, Gonzalo, thank you for listening to me tell you over and over again about the book leaving just enough to the imagination so you would not have to critique me. You do know you are my biggest critic as well as my biggest fan.

My children (Kenith, David, Jeremy, Crislon and Kyleigh) have been such an encouragement to me, and for that I am grateful.

To my mama, (Eleanor Jarriel), thank you for your pride in me and my work. Your encouragement kept me going many a day when I wanted to quit. I could actually feel daddy (Jason Jarriel), and Grandmama (Florrie Kennedy) rooting for me. Even though they are no longer with us, I hope I have somehow made them proud.

I wish to acknowledge my siblings, Gail West, Beth Barnett, Louie Jarriel and Kim Johnson. I wish to thank you for being who you are in your own unique way. Your added wisdom has given me many ideas for other books to follow.

To all my friends, I thank you for your faith in me.

Lastly, thank you David Wiggins, for giving me permission to write this book. You have made us all proud of you for your leadership not only in the community but honoring God and the church after such an experience you had.

Most of all, I thank God—for without Him, nothing could be done—He gave me the desire and also the ability to put my ideas into words. Thank you, Lord.

Sue Garcia

FOREWORD

This piece of work has been in the making starting as a fresh vision some twenty five years ago. I have always been fascinated by the circumstances surrounding what used to be called "The Rattlesnake Roundup". This fascination has led me in wanting to write a book surrounding the circumstances that lead to this event.

Through the misfortune of a family tragedy, I found myself in the same room with David Wiggins. I finally mustered up enough courage to ask him if he would agree for this book to be written. He conceded, and my journey as a first time author and the fulfillment of a lifelong dream had finally begun.

There are only two people still living that were actually involved in the initial incident on that day. These two very important pieces of the puzzle are David himself, the object of this book, and Mr. Preston Clifton, David's uncle. All others who were a part of this story are gone on.

If only the field where the corn was being grown could talk and let us in on the secrets of that day. The old cow barn if not inanimate, could afford a look into the mysteries that led up to this potentially deadly encounter. The field mouse scurrying around the field, thankful that it was not the intended victim, but also long gone, could perhaps have offered some insights.

I have been out to the place where this all happened. Looking at where the old cow barn once stood, and seeing in its place a building used to store fertilizer and the field surrounding it, I have tried to imagine what it was like on that day. I have tried to hear the sounds as they were, and to visualize the different participants and what they went through; the terror they must have felt.

No claim will be made to cover the events exactly as they happened. With the passing of time, some of the memories have begun to fade. One thing is for sure—there was a time, there was a place—a brush with death itself.

Please take time to read the entire book from "cover to cover". The characters in this story are all real, and each plays an important role in the orchestration of the finished product. The pieces of information, however minute one may think they are make for the completeness of the story.

I take pride in this piece of work; I think justice has been done, not perfect by any means, but just the same with heart and fervor.

Sue Garcia

January, 2014

THE BITE

Everyone's story needs to be told, doesn't it? The stories that have been passed down from generation to generation deserve to have at least one listening ear. The news story for the day all the way down to the sweet grandmamma rocking her grand baby and telling a story about a made up land far away land until the toddler's eyes are closed in peaceful rest and contentment. Then there is the story being told when a father and his son enjoy a balmy afternoon sitting on the bank of a river as they enjoy a day of fishing and life changing principles.

So it is with this story. This story that happened in a small town in southeast Georgia almost forty seven years ago is one that also deserves to be told. It has in fact already been told in bits and pieces over and over many times. One person remembers this, another remembers that. Nevertheless, it took place and the events that transpired afterwards has had an everlasting effect on not only the victim, but countless of people living now and for generations to come.

One might compare David Wiggins, small town boy with David, the shepherd boy, later on a king in the Bible. They both faced a terrible giant in their early life as a young lad. As the Bible tells us, the shepherd boy, David, was out in a field tending his father's flocks of sheep. The Philistines had sent a "giant" over to kill the Israelites. Using the power of God on his side, David chose some perfect stones to slay the giant thus saving thousands of lives, and making David a hero in the eyes of the Israelite people.

Centuries later, God once again had his hand on another young boy named David. He too was in a field, and although at the time was so unaware, he would face and slay a giant that had been placed in his path.

Sunday, August 6, 1967, was a day that started off like any other day. Many people had gone to church that morning all over the county. It was no different for David Wiggins and his family. Sunday morning had come and gone, and now Sunday afternoon found some of the family members at one place, and the younger members were enjoying an afternoon of frolicking and playing games with one another. It was a lazy afternoon that was being enjoyed by all members of the family even though they were not together.

Times were hard with a family of six to feed. Many times vegetables were cultivated, picked, and prepared for canning or the freezer. The winter months were more endurable with food that had been prepared and put away for those cold winter nights.

Henry and Pearl Wiggins, along with Preston Clifton and young David, eight years old at the time, had gone out to a garden that was located on the old Dwight Kennedy farm just outside of Claxton, Georgia. Corn and peas were to be picked on that day. The evening had passed on. It was hot as usual for a "dog day" in August. These days happen in late July and August, and are referred to as this because they are described as sultry and hot.

It wouldn't be too long before school started. Wanting to enjoy the last few weeks before he would be told what to wear, David was enjoying being dressed for the day wearing shorts and a tee shirt. He was also barefooted, which is what most of children did in the summertime—go barefoot. On this day, it gave him a true sense of freedom which can be experienced in no other way. Shoes would not have put off what was going to happen no doubt. It may have helped a bit, but probably not too much.

The gnats had been swarming and buzzing around the faces of the corn and pea pickers. Walking up and down the rows of the cornfield with precision produced even more gnats. Not to be discouraged by these creatures, corn was being picked as if nothing was anywhere in the vicinity that would have made a mere fluttering or buzzing sound. The family must work quickly so as to make their trip worthwhile. There would be other hands helping when he returned back home. But for right now, David felt responsible for making his gathering of corn count for something.

He had been solicited by his mom and dad to help with the gathering of the vegetables. He took pride in being the one that was chosen this time to help. He felt like he was a "big man" taking responsibility for his little brothers and sister. He was helping to take care of his family. His role in this procedure was to pick up the corn that his daddy had just broken off from the stalk and thrown to the ground. He obeyed his daddy, and tossed the corn inside the basket that he was carrying.

"Oh be careful little feet where you go, oh be careful little feet where you go, for the Father up above is looking down with love, oh be careful little feet where you go." David had heard this song many times. He had first heard it in Sunday school. He would tap his foot to the beat, and when he sang the line "for the Father up above is looking down with love", he would take his finger and point it up to the sky. Oh how David's feet did go. How he loved to follow behind his daddy, which is just what he was doing on this day. He would go step by step, stride by stride—always being careful to stay inside the footprint of his dad.

Not outside of the print one little bit, but inside so he could be protected not harmed by outside forces. "I'll stay close to Daddy," David thought. One will never know if on this day David did decide to veer off the path of his daddy's shoe print—maybe, maybe not. Besides the scream which came soon thereafter, the next sound that was heard was his daddy shouting, "He's been bit!"

THE AFTERMATH

David had indeed been bitten three times. The rattlesnake was hidden, and hidden very well. Did David really see the snake—probably not. He had felt something though. He wasn't quite sure what it was. He thought maybe it could have been a bee or even a wasp sting. He had even come in contact with a briar patch before while picking blackberries. But this sharp, prickly stab was no comparison to that. It was quick, precise, intended for a specific target. If the bull's eye of that target just happened to be on David's lower extremities, then the mark was well hit.

Besides David's scream which came soon thereafter, the next sound that was heard was his daddy shouting, "Pearl, my God, he's been bitten three times!" While he still had his wits about him, Henry Wiggins reached out to scoop David up in his arms. As he bent down to get him, the snake thrust his slender body which resembled a tire towards him in another attempt to strike again.

She missed, and the same basket that David was using to put the corn in was quickly thrown over the still defensive snake. If it had not been covered up, a most certain verdict would have been another bite to have come quickly after the first three.

Trying again to get both Pearl and Preston's attention, he hollered once more, "He's been bit!" Realizing the gravity in Henry's anguished words, they went to the exact location where he and David were standing just in time to see him put his son on the hood of their pick-up truck.

It didn't take long, and it was soon realized that something had to be done, and done quick. Being a butcher by trade, Henry went right to work, and started making an incision across one of the places where the fangs punctured the skin on David's leg by using what he had on hand—his own pocket knife. He was successful for the first one.

However, this was no hog or cow he was about to cut, but his own flesh and blood. With that thought in mind, he pulled back, and loaded David up to take him to the nearest hospital. Amazingly, the bite that Henry had cut was the one that gave David the least amount of trouble later on.

The corn field was not near the road. To get there, you had to go past the old cow barn, down to where you could see the cows grazing in the grass. They were all down there, but now they must with lightening speed get back to the main road.

With David securely in the truck, and Henry at the wheel, it was Pearl's job to jump off the back of the truck and unlatch each gate. Actually, she didn't just jump off the back of the truck. She was described as "rolling" off the back of the truck. She knew her son's life was at stake.

As the truck went through, she latched the gate shut again. This same repetition was played out over and over again for what seem like an eternity. There was four gates altogether down that long lane or farm vehicle trail. After the fourth gate was securely shut, Henry and his passengers made their way back to where they had left the other children, at their Uncle Preston and Aunt Marjorie's house.

As the truck pulled up in front of the house, Pearl once again "rolled" out of the truck and said, "David's been bit by a snake!" The truck which transported David got to the hospital in approximately eight minutes. The remaining children were loaded up in another vehicle to follow them to the hospital. They anxiously waited outside, not knowing what was going on inside.

David had been carried to what was then known as Dr. Griffin's Clinic. At that time, there was no official hospital in the city of Claxton. This clinic had only two antidotes for snake bites which could only be given with a doctor's approval. There was no doctor on call when David arrived.

There was one doctor who was associated with Dr. Hames' Clinic in Claxton. He would be able to approve this antidote. He was playing golf. He took time to get off of the golf course, and give the orders to expend the medicine. After doing this, he returned to his game of golf.

A call was made to Memorial Hospital in Savannah. The Lord had already prepared them. There just happened to be a doctor completing his internship, and he was specializing in the study of poison. For the first twenty four hours after he had been bitten, David was to be given one shot of the antidote per hour.

It was decided that a transfer to Memorial Hospital would be the best thing to do. It was at this time that finally someone came out of the clinic to tell the siblings what had happened to their big brother, and that he would be going to a bigger hospital some fifty miles away from home.

But that was not before David had died for the first time.

Evans County, Georgia, did not have a hospital back in August of 1967. Due to this, David was loaded up in the local funeral home's 1965 Cadillac S & S hearse. The owners offered their vehicle to the public to make up for the lack of a true ambulance service.

A hearse is what is used to carry the body of a dead person. This one was driven by Murray NeSmith. Colquitt NeSmith, his brother, accompanied him in the passenger's seat. While it was apparent that David's condition was very grave, he certainly was not dead.

Someone asked the ambulance drivers what their incentive was to be going in such a hurry. There was definitely an incentive. It was for the sole purpose of having a chance to save the life of young David Wiggins. His Uncle Charles rode in the ambulance with him. David said to his uncle, "Please don't let me die." His Uncle Preston followed soon thereafter.

When they rounded the corner on Highway 280 by the George Nedar house on the outskirts of Evans County, David felt himself getting nauseous. He broke out into a sweat. He also had chills and a fever. The snake venom was getting into his blood stream, and it was giving him a sickening feeling.

The ambulance started the journey to Savannah, Georgia, on Highway 280. This trip would to take about 55 miles of driving. Interstate 16 was just being built, but it was not yet open. Midway to Savannah, the orange barrels were rolled back, and ambulance and its passengers traveled the rest of the way on the interstate highway. The caravan had a police escort leading the way for them to get through traffic more speedily. David could see the yellow drums and other barricades.

David rose up in the hearse and what he saw gave him the most eerie feeling. The cars were pulled off the road and parked on the sides out of respect. They were waiting for the hearse to pass by. Was it because they had been warned ahead of time that there was a crucial victim inside, or was it because they thought the hearse carried a lifeless body?

Within the span of just a few minutes, David would succumb to death at least two more times.

By the time they made it to the emergency room at Memorial Hospital in Savannah, David's right leg was swollen to the size of his thigh. He went straight to the operating room. Trying to relieve the pressure on his leg, and to also keep it from rupturing, the surgeons made a ten to twelve inch incision on his leg.

After he came out of surgery, he was moved upstairs to intensive care. He was packed in ice from the waist down. The incision stayed open for approximately two weeks and kept in a sterile towel. The doctors had to take skin grafts off of his upper leg. His leg was a very dark color, almost black. He had lost a lot of flesh on his leg.

They put him near the nurses' station so a careful watch could be placed on him. During this time, David heard the nurses say that he was probably going to die. This was a very strong statement for a little eight year old frightened boy to hear.

It was then that he realized that death is real. His mama and daddy told him that he was not going to die. He was going to fight. It was here at the hospital that David became under great conviction about his spiritual well being. He knew he needed to make a decision about his life.

On the following Tuesday, which would have been August 8, 1967, David was again taken to surgery. This time it was for them to amputate his right leg. The doctor encouraged the parents to pray that this would not be the fate that he would have to suffer.

After all was said and done, when David came out of surgery, he still had his leg. He did, however, have to have his three toes amputated. This was a small price to pay for what could have been.

Back then, the rules of the hospital were such that children could not visit the patients. At one time, it was said that Pat Wiggins, David's sister, had asked if her brother had died. Shortly thereafter, her family smuggled her up to the Third Floor Children's Wing to disprove what she thought had happened to him. He was in room 313B of the children's ward; right next to the refreshment center.

Jeffrey and Jerry remember going to see David in the hospital. He pulled back the hospital bed sheet for them to see his leg. It was a big open gap in his leg. His body was black from the waist down.

In January, they did reconstructive surgery on the sole of his foot. He went back to the hospital in the summer of 1968 to have surgery on his foot and toe. He was in the hospital for several months. He went from dying, to having no right leg so he wouldn't be able to walk, and finally to losing three toes. He also had skin grafts.

Many trips were made back to the hospital for therapy. He had to return to the hospital at least once a week. He went to Savannah. During his hospital stay he had four specialists working with him: a pediatrician, a muscle specialist, a snake-bite specialist, and an orthopedic specialist.

When he first went in the hospital, David weighed 100 pounds, and was a stocky fellow. When all was said and done, he had lost a total of thirty pounds, and inherited a much slender build.

To this day, David does walk with a slight limp. He has had some bouts with phlebitis. His leg resembles what would look like the leg of a burn victim with darkening scar tissue that still remains.

While he was in the hospital, David received hundreds of cards and gifts. Many people gave them cash donations, and some doctors didn't charge for their services.

WAS SHE OR WASN'T SHE?

One might not think much about the snake playing a role in this legacy other than being the snake that bit David. However, other than David himself, the snake is the most important component in this situation. Had there not been a snake, there wouldn't have been a bite. Had there not been a bite, David would have just been a normal, run of the mill kid. As it were, there was a snake, and there was certainly a bite. His life was radically changed; forever.

The day David was bitten; all the attention was placed on getting him to the hospital for life saving measures to begin. No one really thought of looking for the snake at the time. Henry did have enough mind about him to situate the vegetable basket on top of the snake that was just waiting to strike anything that decided to step in its path again.

The dramatic scene that had just taken place was now cleared. The main characters in the "would-be" horror story had disbursed. The stillness of the field returned as it was before the sudden episode of terror.

The snake that bit David was doing nothing short of what she should have been doing—protecting her young. She was an Eastern Diamondback Rattlesnake that was for sure. These snakes are the largest rattlesnakes in the world. They are also the most deadly in North America. They are usually four to five feet long. It really would not have made any difference what kind of snake it was, the protection factor would have still be put into place when his foot did indeed come in contact with her.

The cornfield had been the snake's home for quite some time. Some of the leaves on the cornstalks had turned brown. This made it a perfect hiding place and the camouflaged appearance made her fit right in with the scenery . . . Most likely, she was probably about three years old, and had around April of this year finished the lull of wintertime hibernation which is also when the mating process began. In all likelihood, her babies had been born in mid summer.

The vegetable basket which Henry Wiggins had used to put over the snake was still there, but no snake was to be found. Although they weren't right in the vicinity when the episode took place, this particular snake had seven babies which were discovered soon thereafter when Mr. Preston Clifton went back to the location where David had been bitten. The snake and her snakelets were found around an old Volkswagen van.

No one could be certain that is for sure, but it was strongly believed that this snake was the one that had done the irreparable damage to David's leg. At the time, it was thought that there was only one thing that could be done. The snake and her babies must meet their demise. So it was done.

A MOTHER'S LOVE

A mother's love is such that she would do anything within her power for her children. There are times when this motherly love gravitates more toward one child than the other. It does not mean that she loves the other children any less than the chosen one. It just means that at a certain time in the live of this child, she must nurture a little deeper and with a little bit more understanding.

Such was the case in the Wiggins family. David was the first born to Henry and Pearl. There were three other children in the family: Jeffrey, Jerry and Pat. They were all very near in age being less than three years apart. The siblings were close to each other, and there was not anything they would not have done for one another.

After David's encounter with the snake, he became Pearl's center of attention not by choice to neglect the other children, but by obligation to fulfill her motherly duties and desires.

Pearl was one of the last three of fourteen children born in her family. Her father worked with the Seaboard Railroad. Although she wasn't her age, Pearl's younger sister Jessie was able to go to school with her in the same grade. They told Jessie, "If you can learn, you can go to school."

Years later, you could say that Jessie repaid Pearl back for letting her tag along with her at school. While David was in the hospital, she kept his brothers and sisters for her so she could stay at the hospital with him. Pearl wanted to be as close to David as she could, and for as long as it was necessary.

The two sisters were still very close in so many ways. They were very close indeed, and remained that way throughout their adult life. They were both married the same day on June 8, 1958.

Pearl Wiggins had a blue volks wagon which they called "the blue bug". Many times when David had to go back and forth to the hospital in Savannah, she would put his wheelchair in the front. This was so there could be room for not only David, but also for his brothers and sister.

When they got home from one of the many doctor appointments, Pearl would let Jeffrey, Jerry and Pat spin David around in his wheelchair. They were trying to make the best of a very bad situation. They not only loved David, but looked up to him as their big brother. The accident probably made David grow up and feel like he had to be responsible for those younger than he.

On several occasions when his brothers and sister went with her to carry David to Savannah, they would stop back by one of their favorite eating places and get a mini hamburger at Krystals.

Pearl was very protective of David as all mamas not only could be, but should be. She was also very supportive of him, and it is because of her love that he was able to get through this terrible ordeal. Pearl was always there trying her best to hold the family together.

A FATHER'S DEDICATION

Henry Wiggins was one of eight children. He certainly knew what hard work was all about. His daddy, George Wiggins, was one of those last farmers that cultivated his crops with a mule drawn plow, and Henry clearly inherited some of those same hard working ethics from him. Henry was a self-taught man with an eighth grade education.

Before David got bit, Henry Wiggins was living the American dream. One of the happiest times for him was when he purchased a Cadillac. He had been taking care of his family the best way he knew how, and seemed to be doing a fairly good job of it.

The family had moved from Metter, Georgia, when David was about five years old. Henry ran a grocery store in Hagan on the corner of Fire tower Road and Highway 280. Then hard times started coming their way. An electrical fire had started and burned the store and all the contents inside. Henry had to start over. The family was displaced and had to move in with some relatives for approximately one year.

It was during the time that David got bit by the snake that Henry had to take on three jobs to keep the family afloat. He got a job on the road selling wholesale meats. He also had a route where he sold tires. In addition, he had a country ham business. Later on, when a local gas station had blown up, Henry used that space to open up a fruit and vegetable stand.

Pearl stayed very close to David's side, so Henry had to make up for the difference of Pearl not working.

The hospital bills were mounting up, and times were very hard. They were thousands of dollars for David's hospital stay alone. David's mom and dad had no medical insurance. They went through "the storm" when he was sick.

They lost the house to foreclosure. It was sold to the same man that Henry had purchased it from. This man was such a friend that he continued to let the Wiggins live in it, rent free. About a year later, Henry was able to re-purchase the house—this time for keeps.

Anyone who has ever had the opportunity to own a vehicle knows what it feels like to have that special, one of a kind, irreplaceable car or truck. Such was the case with the blue truck that was owned by Henry Wiggins. He loved that truck. It was what one might say was his "pride and joy."

In retrospect this truck was purchased by money that was well spent although this was not known at the time. This same truck would be one of the many devices that were used to help the family through a very devastating time in their lives.

After the hospital bills started mounting up, he was forced to sell the items. The truck that Henry so dearly loved had to be sold. Albert Threet purchased the truck from him to help out in a time of need. The boat was also sold.

It was along this time that Henry started selling rose bushes. This small time business soon would be what was later known as Wiggins' Florist and Garden Center. He bought azaleas from a place in Hinesville.

HOMECOMING AND COMMUNITY SUPPORT

After the inevitable long stay in the hospital in Savannah, Georgia, David was finally dismissed to come home to family, friends, acquaintances, classmates and a community of well wishers. This collaboration would prove to be an integral part of his recovery process.

When David was released from the hospital, there was an outpouring of love and compassion from everyone. The community got together and some ladies from the factory bought him a new bicycle. The doctor had told them that this would be good exercise for David as he started to use his leg again. For some of the workers, this was a full week's pay.

Someone in the community gave a desk to him so he could do his school work even when he could not attend school.

Eastside Baptist Church, under the direction of Pastor Felton Moseley, headed up an effort to raise money for David's hospital expenses. They set up contribution stations at the church, Bowen-Rogers Hardware, The Claxton Bank and Bill Colson's Grocery.

The family who was left at home sometimes had to stay at different houses. Everyone pitched in and helped take care of the children. Friends and church family members brought food to the hungry family after a day at school or coming home from a hard day at work.

People in the community kept David's brothers and sister while Henry and Pearl went to the hospital in Savannah. They would always come home to a hot meal that was prepared for them so they wouldn't have to do that when they got home.

Now a grown man, David recalls that going to the first roundup as being very nervous. A lot of folks were curious and wanted to see his leg and hear his story. David shared his story many times.

SCHOOL DAYS

The school David attended was Claxton Elementary School in Claxton, Georgia. This school was located right on Main Street. The building was a two story brick and nostalgia in structure. Mrs. Doris Sands was David's first grade teacher. Mrs. Joyce Nesmith taught him second grade.

David was a very sweet child so says Mrs. Frances Hodges, his third grade teacher. There were to be three third grade classes that year. The three teachers drew names to see which students would be on their class roll. She drew David's name out.

After his life threatening mishap, she took his lessons and books to him. He listened very well. His mama went over the lessons with him at night. She had David read the newspaper. David would not only be making gains in his reading fluency, he would also be keeping up with what was happening in the world.

The most memorable comment that Mrs. Hodges made about him was, "I had no doubt that he would be able to do this." By saying that, she meant that he would be able to accomplish whatever it was he needed to do in order to pass third grade. She had faith in him even though he was going to be missing a lot of days from school.

When he came home from the hospital, he went to school for one half of the day. He would get very sluggish and sleepy. After Christmas, David was able to stay the entire day at school except when he had to miss occasionally for a trip to the doctor.

Mrs. Gwen Strickland was David's fourth grade teacher. When you entered the main doors to the school - the doors that front on Highway 280, her room was the first one on the right. When he started this grade, David was on crutches. By the end of the school year, he had transitioned into a brace. In those days, the buildings were not air conditioned. If a student was the helper for the day, it was his job to let the windows up and down so the students could stay cool.

This particular time, the windows had to be propped open because the weights had fallen off of them. Being the good helper that he was, David was trying to open the window one morning. Looking back, he now realizes that he should have waited for help. Being the independent fellow he was, he wanted to do it all by himself. This was not such a good idea.

The window was about half way open. He had tried to prop it up before he could open it up the rest of the way. Unfortunately, the window fell on him, and caught his middle finger on the right hand between the window and the window sill.

David screamed. Mrs. Strickland came and opened the window. David screamed again as he made his way to the office bleeding as he went. After all was said and done, he had to go to the doctor and have his finger sewn up. Needless to say, David didn't want to the helper in the classroom for a long time after that episode.

Some of David's childhood classmates and friends were Donna Nesmith Durrence, Michelle Smith Tootle, Angie

Smith Miller, Gina Threet Roberts, Greg Threatte, Ann Thompson Webb, Joey McNeely, Jody Sikes, and Eddie Akins.

David may have never been a king in real life. He was, however, King Potato along with Gena Threet, one of his classmates, who played the part of Queen Potato . They crouched down behind some cardboard boxes to present a show for their excited classmates to watch.

During this year, his grade level put on a play in front of the entire school. It was a big deal to be chosen to do this. The name of the play was "Jack and the Beanstalk". David and some of his friends were in the play as well.

Mrs. Kennedy was the music teacher and she helped with the play. Michelle Smith played the part of Jack's mom. David, being the stocky boy that he was, happened to be assigned the role of the giant. He learned his part very well. He also had to sing. It was the only time that anyone at school asked him to sing a solo - this was also the last time.

Not wanting to be a soloist, David tried his hand at playing in the band. His instrument was the coronet/trumpet. He started playing in the fifth grade, and continued playing until he was a junior in high school. Mel Kelley was his band director.

"Hop" Perkins was the Police Chief for the City of Hagan. He knew that little boys always dream of riding in the back of a patrol car. He helped David and some of his friends make that dream come true.

After school, perhaps after he had finished directing traffic or cruising through the town, he would pick up David and his friends, put them in the back of the patrol car, and take them on a ride to the store to buy some candy. What young man wouldn't be thrilled with an adventure like that?

David started off fifth grade wearing a boot brace. It was also this year that he got to take this off. This was certainly a good thing because David loved football. This year he was on the " Black Bears" team. There were four teams. The coaches for the team were Bobby Kennedy, Daryl Thompson and Bryon Haire. He continued playing in the sixth and seventh grades.

This was all done without a doctor's permission. He was a very determined young man. For some reason, he decided he would end his football career in the seventh grade, but while he was a part of the team he gave it everything he had within him.

David was a part of the debate team in high school. Other students on team were Linny Bailey, Keith Sapp, and Cecil Murphy. The sponsor for the team was Mr. John Frazier. He was also their history teacher. This team won the sub region and the region debates.

When they went to the state competition, they felt in their hearts that they would be out classed. When they arrived, they found out that there were only four teams participating in the debate. The Claxton team came in fourth, so that was what they decided to tell everyone back home. Until now, they hadn't told anyone that there were only four teams in the competition that day.

There was trouble brewing when David got to be a senior in high school. As Senior Class President, David enjoyed a great relationship with the principal, Mr. Dewey Hulsey.

Mr. Frazier and Mr. Herb Driver, other high school teachers, suggested that David make out a purchase order for a case of dynamite and blasting caps for the senior class to purchase.

The idea was that when Mr. Hulsey signed the purchase order, the class would have some fun with him. They never really intended to purchase the items requested. However, the plan backfired, because someone had already alerted Mr. Hulsey to this little scheme, so he decided to have some fun with them.

Mr. Hulsey called David into his office. He told him that such an offense would warrant a unique punishment. Throughout that senior year, he would constantly remind David that he was still working on his punishment. He would tell him to remember that "every dog has its day".

On Honor's Day, he made David stand up, and once again reminded him that "every dog has its day". Not many people knew what was going on. On graduation day, inside David's folder, in place of a high school diploma, there was a certificate which said, "We do hereby award this certificate to David Wiggins for barely making it."

David went to Mr. Hulsey and asked him about his diploma. Mr. Hulsey simply told him "that if he could not run with the big dogs, then stay on the porch." He also told him that "another year of high school would probably do the trick."

He dangled him on for a while, and when Mr. Hulsey realized how anxious David was getting he informed him that his diploma was inside the back cover. David did not pick on Mr. Hulsey again. He had learned his lesson.

ADVENTURES WITH CHILDHOOD FRIENDS

The snake bite was not the first time David had trouble with this right leg. During the summer between first and second grade, he and his friends decided they would play "Super Heroes" with David being Superman himself. This impersonation involved jumping off the roof of a house. He had already been told by his parents not to be anywhere near there, so trouble was bound to happen, and happen it did!

This store building was behind Sikes Abattoir, which was an animal slaughter house in Hagan, Georgia. David's friend had already taken his turn jumping off the roof, and now it was David's turn.

His friend told him that since he was Superman, he should be able to jump with no problems. Just before David was to jump, the friend moved the ladder. David took him at his word, and jumped. Needless to say, when David jumped, his "superman" powers didn't show up. He fell to the ground flat as a pancake.

A young man gave him a ride home. He told David that he certainly hoped his leg was not broken. When David asked him why, he simply told him that they do the same thing to humans just like they do to horses with a broken leg. They "put them down" or shoot them to get them out of their misery. For that reason, he sure hoped that David's leg was not broken.

David certainly did not want to tell his mom and dad about him supposedly breaking his leg. Not only did he not want to get into trouble for disobeying his parents, but more importantly, he did not want to be put down. He did not have any supper that evening. He was too scared to eat.

This frightened little boy, only in second grade, spent the night on the couch. There was no sleep for David that night. He agonized and writhed in pain from his leg, but refused to wake his mama and daddy up for fear of what the consequences might be.

The next morning he told his mama that he could not walk because his leg hurt him so bad. His mama took him to the Griffin Hospital in Claxton. This was the same hospital that he would later go to for the snake bite. They took an x-ray of his leg, and it indeed was broken. The doctor was amused to think that David thought he was going to be shot because of his leg being broken.

GOD MEANT IT FOR GOOD

David's Aunt Lois' pastor came to see him while he was in the hospital. He impressed on him about his need for salvation. He told him that by all odds, he should have died, but yet he lived. He also told him that he should wonder why death did not happen to him. He then asked him that if he had died, where he thought he would have spent eternity. Not long after this, David told his mom that he wanted to see a pastor about his salvation.

The Bible stories that David learned in church as a young boy really did make a difference. He fondly remembers Mrs. Marjorie Rogers teaching him at Eastside Baptist Church in Claxton. Her flannel graph stories always brought the characters of the Bible to life.

Little did he know then that things like this would be setting the stage for years to come of what he was meant to do and become. The impressions that were made on him during his youth made him stronger after he suffered his mishap.

Before his daddy's store burned, David worked everyday after school and on Saturdays. He didn't know it then, but he would one day work in the public realm. He might not ever become the president of the United States, but God certainly had some political ideas in mind for him.

When he was only in the first or second grade, while working at his dad's store, he was a campaign manager and didn't even know it. He would tell folks as they came in and out of the store that they should vote for Lester Mattox, who was then a candidate for the highest office in the State of Georgia. Well, as it happened, Mr. Mattox did go on to become the Governor of Georgia. One would like to think that the campaigning that David did helped him win the race.

Someone made sure that Governor Mattox knew about David and his snake bite. They told the Governor that David had been a campaign manager for him in his local hometown. Mr. Mattox was very appreciative of the work that David had done for him. He showed his appreciation by sending him a personal letter while he was in the hospital. David also received a letter from Senator Joe Kennedy.

David later became the senior class president at Claxton High School. He was the President of the Chamber of Commerce and also the Industrial Development Authority at the same time. It would seem that he may have taken on too much, but he was dedicated to every task he took ownership of.

In addition to all of this, David was the mayor of Hagan, Georgia, for two terms. He got elected when he was twenty seven years old, and he resigned when he was thirty five years old.

Jeremiah 29:11 says, "For I know the plans I have for you," declares the Lord, "plans to prosper you and not to harm you, plans to give you hope and a future." It appeared that God did indeed have something good in mind for David and his family.

Where the old cow barn used to be. This is the location where David was bitten by the rattle snake.

Ambulance/Hearse that David rode in to the hospital

Mr. Preston Clifton holding the snake that is
believed to have been the one that bit David. The
smaller snake was one of her snake lets.

The truck used to carry David to the hospital. It
was later sold to help pay for hospital bills.

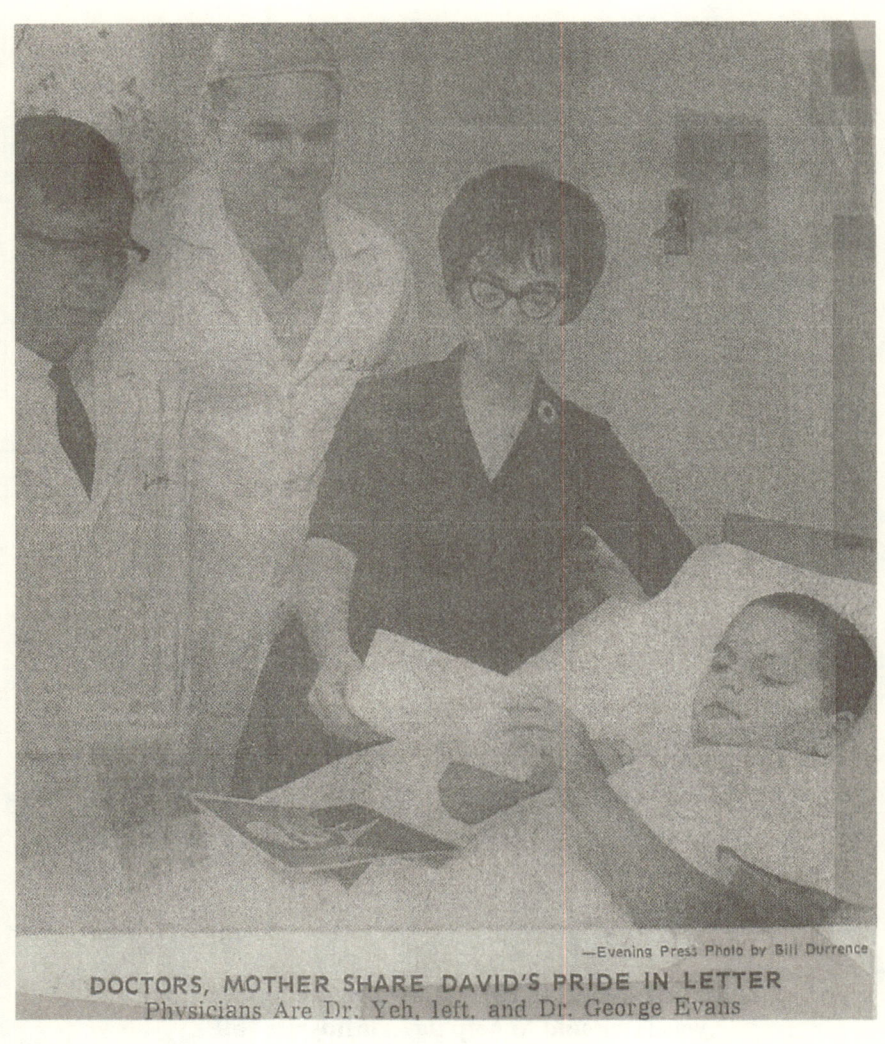

-Evening Press Photo by Bill Durrence

DOCTORS, MOTHER SHARE DAVID'S PRIDE IN LETTER
Physicians Are Dr. Yeh, left, and Dr. George Evans

**David reading the letter that Gov. Lester
Mattox had written to him.**

Office of the Governor
Atlanta

August 14, 1967

Master David Wiggins, Jr.
Memorial Medical Center
Room 301
Savannah, Georgia

Dear David:

I regret to learn that you are hospitalized from being bitten by a rattler but I am delighted that you are on the road to recovery again. I believe you are the only Campaign Manager I ever had who was bitten three times by a snake. One question please... did you bite the snake back?

Seriously, David, I am very proud of you and your school record. I am sure that a bright young man like you will soon catch up again once you are back in school. Try not to think about being behind and just concentrate on getting well again. Will you do that for me?

I want to personally commend you on attending Sunday School and Church regularly on Sunday and I am sure that God will bless you and help you to get well and strong again very soon.

David, thank you so much for all the help you gave me during my campaign. I am more than happy to send you a photograph of me because you helped me to get elected.

Let me hear from you and how you are getting along. With every good wish for your speedy recovery, I am

Sincerely your friend,

Lester Maddox

LM/jp

David received a letter from Gov. Lester Mattox

JOSEPH E. KENNEDY
Fourth District
206 New Drive
Claxton, Georgia 30417

COMMITTEES

AGRICULTURE & NATURAL RESOURCES
APPROPRIATIONS
EDUCATIONAL MATTERS
PENAL & CORRECTIONAL AFFAIRS

The State Senate

Atlanta, Georgia

August 22, 1967

Mr. David Wiggins
Memorial Medical Center
Savannah, Georgia

Dear David:

Just a note to wish you a speedy recovery from your unfortunant accident. I have been real concerned and have been following your progress through mutual friends of ours.

Friends are a wonderful thing and you are blessed with s o very many who are concerned about you and your welfare. Hurry and get well as I know you are anxious to return home.

Give my regards to your Mother & Father and If I can be of any s ervice to you, please call on me.

Sincerely,

JOSEPH E. KENNEDY

JEK/s

The State Senate
Atlanta, Georgia
JOSEPH E. KENNEDY
Fourth District
206 New Drive
Claxton, Ga. 30417

David received a letter from Senator Joe Kennedy

(Back) Left to right: Jerry, David, Jeffrey
(Front) Left to right: Pat, Pearl, Henry

David liked to play his guitar to pass the time. Notice the cards and "get-well" wishes in the background.

A picture of David on cow with his cousin Bill Clifton

David as he attended one of the Rattlesnake Roundups

1969 Season—
Midget League

THE BLACK BEARS — On the Bear roster are Allen Horton, Phil Smith, Bobby Hodges, Mike Griffin, Sammy Lott, Barry Kennedy, Cliff Kennedy, Mark Eason, Robert Jenkins, Bill Collins, Byron Haire, David Anderson, Eric Engstron, David Waters, Jerry Rustin, Gary Crosby, Donald Crosby, Scott Griffin, Jody McNeely, Sammy Doster, Dave Tippins, David Wiggins, Eric Brewton, and Dwayne Kirkland. Coaches are Darrell Thompson and Bobby Kennedy.

David in his "Preacher Suit"

**David as the Grand Marshall in the
Rattlesnake Roundup Parade**

David's picture as he pursued the political field

The Rev. David Wiggins, right, has been called as the pastor of Circle Hill Baptist Church in Sneads. He stands with his wife, Cindy, left; son, Dave, back center; and daughter, Kim.

David and his young family as he accepts the position of a pastor

A SPECIAL CALLING

David didn't let the obstacle of the near death experience captivate and hold him in its clutches. God had already devised a plan for him. Maybe David knew it, maybe not. Perhaps he knew that he was to pursue life with everything he had within him. After all, he was given a new lease on life.

David had spoken to his pastor, Mr. Felton Moseley, about his admitted need for a savior. He gave his life to Jesus on October 8, 1967, and was baptized on November 26, 1967.

Both David and Cindy Sapp went to Eastside Baptist Church. When they first met, she didn't know that he was the fellow who had been bitten by the snake. When she found out, it had no bearings on how she felt about him.

He and Cindy started dating. He didn't have a license, but still drove to pick Cindy up. They dated for three years and then got married on October 22, 1977. At this time, Cindy worked at Georgia Pacific Corporation, and David worked at Wiggins Landscaping.

David went from being a youth in the church, to a youth teacher when he was just nineteen years old. For seventeen years, he was a youth leader and youth pastor. Although they were serving God, they felt he was calling them to do something else.

When God calls a man, He doesn't just call him, but he calls his entire family. One evening David knelt down by his loveseat praying and searching for God's wisdom and will for his life. God revealed to David what His will was for him. He wanted him to go to Bible College to become a minister. David told God He would have to work on Cindy.

Both David and Cindy had been involved in moving other couples to Graceville, Florida, where there was a Bible college.

When David revealed to Cindy what he thought God's will was for them, Cindy let David know that God had not revealed that to her.

Eventually they went for a visit to Graceville to the Bible College. God was very gracious, and the decision for them to leave Claxton to go to strange territory was confirmed, and thus their journey in the ministry had begun.

David could not tell his church family at Eastside Baptist until he had broke the news to his Daddy. He had just suffered a heart attack, and had by-pass surgery.

Funds were needed for their move to Graceville, and God did supply these in ways beyond one's comprehension. David had a curbing machine. He had taken out a loan, and needed $7,500 to get out from under it. God provided that money in seventy five one hundred dollar bills.

On April 13th, they got their income tax. After paying the bills, they had $150.00 left over. On August 1, 1994, they moved to Graceville. Eastside Baptist Church sent support money. David and Cindy leased their house for extra income.

When the Lord gives you a chance to do something that your heart yearns to do, it is scary not to do it. It's with these risks that we learn to walk in faith.

They did make it to the Bible College in Graceville, Florida. David went on to study theology at Southern Baptist Theological Seminary and Florida Baptist Theological College.

He went on to become the pastor of churches in Georgia and in Kentucky. He has been the pastor of Lewis Lane Baptist Church in Owensboro, Kentucky since 2008.

According to David himself, the greatest thing that has come out of this entire ordeal is his salvation. The best thing that came out of it for our community was the sense that we look out for one another. "Cindy and I have lived in a lot of different places since we left Claxton in 1994, but the familiarity and sense of community that Evans County has is not to be dismissed or devalued. When our times were difficult, the very best in our community and in the hearts of folks came out."

There's something fascinating about looking eye to eye with a rattlesnake. The Wildlife Festival is the biggest monetary event that happens in Evans County. People will come from miles around just to look at one of these snakes.

Keith Barnard, President

Evans County Wildlife Club

David was my youth pastor at Eastside Baptist Church. When I had just turned the age where I was ready to take some driving lessons. One lesson I was taking took me to our driveway and subsequently towards our carport. As I started under the carport, I ran right into our grill.

The next time we gathered together at church, David held up a giant poster that read "Save the Grill". Needless to say, I will always remember him for not only this, but also being a great youth pastor.

Christy Tucker Dyson

David Wiggins was my youth pastor at Eastside Baptist Church. I remember him as being a very godly man. He taught me many things while he was my youth leader, but the one thing I will always remember is his value of time.

Whenever we went on a trip of any kind—it didn't matter how far, or how long it took to get there, David would always say, "we'll be there in about five minutes"!

Deana Cameron Floyd

DAVID WIGGINS

My first recollections of David Wiggins were when he and I started our elementary school experience in Ms. Doris Sand's first grade class. I recall thinking how funny his last name sounded which is quite interesting when you consider that mine is Threatte. He and I became good friends very quickly when we learned that we lived just across the branch from each other in the town of Hagan where he would later be elected and serve as Mayor.

The friendship he and I shared took on a new meaning when during the summer from school David has the misadventure of having an all too close encounter with an Eastern Diamond Back. I, along with all of my classmates for the next several months awaited word on his condition and recovery and often the entire class would make cards that would be taken to him in the hospital. Being so young, I don't recall the length of recovery or when he was finally able to return to school. I do know that as soon as he had recovered enough our active friendship resumed and was the case in those days, we were in the streets of Hagan playing together until sundown.

We remained very close throughout our entire school career through Elementary, Jr. High, and High School. David was instrumental in getting me my first job working with him in his Dad's Landscape supply business. He and I would work in the Nursery Center's greenhouses and nursery and would occasionally go to job sites to install plants and sprig sod. I recall a large job we worked on what for Roger's Funeral Home which is not the site of Evans County Board of Education.

David always presented himself as a leader which garnered him the election to our Senior Class President. Those leadership skills would serve him well in years to come as he was elected to serve as Mayor of Hagan. Having become a very strong Christian, David also surrendered to the Call to the Ministry and began his studies which would prepare him for a Church leadership role as Pastor.

Recent years have placed miles between us however that friendship continues albeit through the venue of Social

Media. David has long been an inspiration to me in the way he handled trials encountered which I am confident was God's preparing him for the Pastorate way back in Elementary School.

Greg Threatte

In the spring of 1999, I was asked to participate in the Rattlesnake Roundup Pageant. This has always been a big deal in our area for as long as I can remember. If you are a female living in Evans County during your senior year of high school, this is something that you anticipate. It is considered an honor by most. Now, I am not beauty pageant material. I had never participated in any type of beauty pageant in my life. When I was initially asked, I was unsure if this was something that I personally wanted to do. I have nothing against beauty pageants, but I wasn't a "girly girl" and felt like it was out of my comfort zone. Of course, my parents were thrilled and basically told me that I would do it. So, it was with great hesitation that I accepted the nomination and proceeded down the beauty pageant road.

Once I accepted the nomination, I was quickly put to work. I immediately started having personal meetings with Mrs. Henrietta Rogers. She has to be the most proper lady I have ever met, but also one of the sweetest. Mrs. Henrietta has the most patience! I was raised in the country on dirt roads and tractors. Mrs. Henrietta wanted me to walk like I was "walking on cotton and clouds." I needed to hold my shoulders back, stand up straight, and smile all at the same time. She really had her work cut out with me. But, I will admit, when I was at her studio, I felt like a princess. She always found something I was doing right, something I was improving upon. She made a little country girl from Daisy feel like a queen. I thought going to her practices was going to be a painful experience, but it turned out to be something I looked forward too. I still see Mrs. Henrietta around town, and I get excited. I developed a real respect for her and still just look at her and think—wow. I really have no other words to describe her. I would love to be more like her in so many ways. But all I can say is—wow.

As the pageant got closer we began meeting at PCA and practicing on stage. This is when it really hit home that I was going to be in a real beauty pageant! I had to buy a dress, get my hair done, and wear make-up. The practices were a lot of fun because many of my childhood friends were also in the pageant. We would giggle a lot at each other on stage and just really have a lot of fun together. We also had to decorate the float for the parade. This is a big deal because it's televised. The Roundup parade is by far the biggest parade for Evans County. Everyone comes to it.

The pageant literally took two days because we had interviews on Friday afternoon, the pageant Friday night, the parade Saturday morning, and the snake hunt Saturday morning, not to mention a breakfast at Mrs. Patricia Bell's house. After all of that, it was off to the warehouse! I will never forget the interview session. It was held at the Public Library. I was scared to death. Each contestant is taken in a room with an interview panel and asked a series of questions. As nerve racking as it was, the interview team was so kind. They tried their best to make each of us feel comfortable. Upon surviving that, it was off to the pageant. I will never forget that night. For that one night, I truly did feel like a queen. Crown or no crown, everyone involved in the pageant made you feel like you were the winner. It was so much fun. I even wondered, "Are all pageants this much fun? Have I really missed out on something by refusing to be in previous pageants?" I was told by veteran pageant participants that all pageants are not that fun. The Rattlesnake Roundup Pageant is different. It makes each girl feel special. Each participant walks away with a renewed sense of pride in who they are and a pride in being part of Evans County. Saturday morning starts very early the day of the Roundup. All the girls met at Mrs. Patricia Bell's house. Now, this is another sweet lady that holds a special place in my heart. She worked so hard to prepare a wonderful breakfast for the contestants. We were able to be silly and get rid of a lot of our jitters at her house that morning. Jitters you ask? Well, after eating breakfast, we all loaded a school bus and went on a real snake hunt. Yep, in our finest clothes, we went walking through the woods, hunting rattlesnakes. I must admit, it was quite an experience. Of course, the men in the wildlife club, being the expert snake hunters they were, found a gopher hole within minutes. It was long before they pulled a huge rattlesnake out of the hole for all of us to see.

After the snake hunt, we quickly made our way to CHS to begin our parade. We all jumped on the float and began the parade route. Back in those days the number of people who came from literally all over to the roundup and parade was unbelievable. The roads were lined with people throughout the route. Everyone was waving and cheering. Once again, we all felt like winners. We were all made to feel equally important. The parade was cold that year, but I still remember where I sat on the float, who I sat beside, and the feeling I had riding through town with everyone waving at us. It was so much fun.

The queen wasn't announced until around 2:00 on Saturday afternoon. This gave the contestants time to be bused to the warehouse and access to the snake pit. Oh yes, the snake pit. Each contestant was taken into the snake pit, shown how to milk the snakes, and allowed to hold one of the rattlesnakes. Now, I wasn't going to pass up this chance. I still have my picture to this day of me with a huge rattlesnake. It was awesome! Well, after all of the fun in the snake pit, the girls take the stage to find out who is going to be crowned queen and princess. At that point in the day, I had already had so much fun I honestly didn't care if I won or not. I was so glad I had listened to my parents and participated in this once in a lifetime experience. You know, you don't have many once in a lifetime experiences, but this was clearly one of them when you think about it.

I wasn't officially named Miss. Rattlesnake Roundup Queen or Princess that year. I didn't even get Miss Congenitally. I'm perfectly ok with that. I believe I gained so much through the whole experience. I learned so much about myself as well as many others in our community. I was able to establish lasting relationships with ladies in our community that I still treasure to this day. I learned a lot about the history of my county that I probably would have never otherwise learned. But the most important thing I learned was that anyone can be made to feel special. I learned that everyone needs to feel special, feel pretty, to feel like they are worthy. Even if it's just for one weekend, it lasts a lifetime. All of the people involved in putting on this pageant make it their goal to make each contestant feel all of these things and so much more. These are memories I will continue to treasure throughout my life. I have never told the Wildlife Club members thank you, but I truly am thankful for the experience and will always cherish it.

—Sarah Rountree

After the surprise sunk in, I was absolutely honored to be crowned the 1981 Rattlesnake Roundup Queen. At that time, both juniors and seniors were invited to compete for the crown. I was a junior at Pinewood Christian Academy. I remember clearly the rattlesnake hunt and going into the snake pit. Even though I have a fear of snakes, I held the body of an eastern diamondback rattlesnake . . . of course while the handler had the head. My year as Miss Rattlesnake Roundup provided me with many opportunities to serve as public relations for both the annual Roundup and Evans County. I visited many local area festivals, attended many pageants, and rode in numerous parades. There were many interesting questions posed and many acquaintances met as I represented the Wildlife Club. The Evans County Wildlife Club was very gracious to my family and me. I was invited to their family night suppers and given a club jacket to wear. I made many wonderful memories and friends during my reign. Many years have passed, but the Wildlife Club is always remembering the past queens with invitations to their parade, pageant, Queen Activities, and the Roundup itself. I will never forget the opportunity that was given to me and the Wildlife Club will always be near to my heart. Some of the club members I remember so dearly have since passed, but the club continues to honor the legacy they were left with to carry forward.

—Kathryn Sutton

The year was 1971. I was a senior at Claxton High anxiously anticipating graduation in June. When the invitation was issued to me to participate in the Rattlesnake Roundup activities that year I was excited and humbled. I was excited to be chosen to be involved with such a worthwhile event and humbled that the members of the Evans County Wildlife Club would believe that I might be a worthy representative for the club's Rattlesnake Roundup.

The process for being named Roundup Queen was quite a bit different "back then". The contestants met the wildlife club members at a meal in our honor and then the members voted by secret ballot. I know beauty and talent did not get me selected as winner but it meant a lot to me to be chosen by a group of my community leaders who really knew who I was and voted on mine and my family's personalities and reputations. Most of them had known me, and I them, most of my life.

The crowning was on the Saturday of the Roundup activities at the Claxton Tobacco Warehouse. The morning activities before the crowning were really enjoyable, educational and a bit eerie. It was a lot of fun to go on the Snake Hunt and ride in the parade with my friends and fellow queen contestants. On the hunt we were able to see the procedures used to hunt, find and catch the snakes. Nothing that was done seemed to be cruel to the animals especially knowing that the venom extracted from them later would be used to save lives. The hunters let us listen to the "singing" sounds of the rattler down in the hole. I still get terrified if I hear that noise—but thank goodness I learned what that noise was!

I did take, and have since taken, a few friendly teases about being the "Snake Queen". But that never has really seemed like a derogatory name to me. I am really proud to have been able to be a part of this event that was started because of David Wiggin's run-in with one of these deadly snakes. The Wildlife Club has always done an excellent job in educating people about how rattlesnakes operate and how people need to respect them and their territory. I am afraid some of that may have been lost in the recent years of restrictions that some organizations have forced on the club.

Because I went to church with David for a long time and knew his family well, the Roundup has a little stronger impact on me. Around Roundup time each year, and other times it is brought up, I think about what could have happened to David had help not been gotten. I watched David grow to be a godly man and he has influenced many people with his sweet spirit and the Word of the Lord. I am so thankful for the attempts of the Wildlife Club to make people more aware of the dangers and the benefits of these often deadly vipers. It truly is an honor and a privilege to be able to say I am a part of an event that is such a tradition and heritage of Evans County.

—Pam Todd

Mr. Danny Strickland and myself were the first the start— also Jack Tucker. The first time we went snake hunting, we went to Groveland, Georgia. The grass was about waist high. We got four snakes.

There were about a dozen members at the Wildlife Club to begin with. We first met at Kicklighter's shop in Claxton. We went snake hunting every Saturday and Sunday.

We went snake hunting everywhere including Carson Sands' property.

On the Jernigan's property, we caught seven snakes. We put the snakes in the back of the truck. A state patrol stopped us. He left without checking it. Danny, Mike and Danny Todd caught the most snakes at Hagan Bay. We always caught snakes there.

Gary Tippins and Fred Daniel told me and Danny that they went behind Kildays horse farm. They put up a sign saying "we're here, come on in". We drove through the water. We drove the truck out, and took the fan belt off and went on through.

We soon bought the Wildlife Club from Johnny Clark. It was on the river.

We went from having the Roundup at the Claxton Tobacco Warehouse to Hagan, Georgia. Lex Strickland wanted to sell the warehouse. The oil company needed a building.

Billy Odom

January, 2013

THE FIRST RATTLESNAKE ROUNDUP

The first Rattlesnake Roundup which was held on February 24, 1968, was an interesting experience. Who in the world would think about catching rattlesnakes for any reason?

The idea was brought to my attention, as president of Evans County Wildlife Club, by Ernest Strickland who was a member of Farm Bureau. He was concerned about the growing number of rattlesnakes in this area. His concern about the rattlesnake population was kindled by the youth, David Wiggins, being bitten by a rattlesnake in the summer of 1967.

Mr. Strickland approached me as president of the Evans County Wildlife Club about staging a Rattlesnake Roundup. My response was, "A what!" Mr. Strickland said that he had heard that the town of Whigham, Georgia, was scheduled to have a Rattlesnake Roundup in January, 1968. We decided to go to Whigham to see how they held their Roundup. Ernest

Strickland, Kenneth Durrence, Farm Bureau President, B. E. Smith, Sr. and I traveled to Whigham, Georgia, to the Roundup.

Due to my concern of having a Roundup in about three weeks, we decided it would be a good idea to have the Farm Bureau and the Wildlife Club co-sponsor this event. Thus it was decided that Ernest Strickland and I would be co-chairmen of this event. We learned from our visit to the Whigham Roundup that Roundups should be held when the temperatures are coldest since the snakes would be less active at that time. Therefore, we decided to stage the Roundup on Saturday, February 17, 1968. This would give us approximately three weeks to organize the event. It was decided to have the Roundup on the vacant lot across from the Evans County Health Department on Newton and Liberty Streets.

We built three pens out of fine mesh wire and wood floors and then we placed a layer of sand in the bottom of the pens. These pens were enclosed by another fence which prevented spectators from getting too close to the snakes. As the Roundup date drew nearer, it was determined that the snake hunters needed additional time to catch more snakes. The Roundup date was changed to Saturday, February 24, 1968. Due to sleet and snow on the day of the Roundup, it was moved to the Planters Tobacco Warehouse.

As plans for the Roundup were being made, a local resident, Amos Thompson, who was a serviceman for Georgia Power came to me and said that he knew how to catch rattlesnakes. He had been catching snakes since 1932. He was invited to come to the Wildlife Club meeting to demonstrate his method of catching rattlesnakes. Mr. Thompson was also asked if he would present a "rattlesnake milking" and snake handing demonstration at the Roundup. He agreed to do this.

Senator Joe Kennedy and Representative Hines Brantley were on the program at the first Roundup.

There was 48 snakes brought in with prizes given as follows the person from Evans County with the most snakes, the person (other than Evans County), with the most snakes, the biggest snake by weight, and the longest snake. The snake hunters were paid $3 a piece for each snake.

This was an exciting experience for everyone! No one ever dreamed that the event would grow to the magnitude which it is today.

I commend the Evans County Wildlife Club for their accomplishments.

Bill Hearn

March, 2001

THE EVANS COUNTY WILDLIFE CLUB

The Evans County Wildlife Club is located on the Canoochee River, east of Highway 301, on approximately one acre of land purchased by the Club in 1979.

Membership into the Club (both active and honorary) is by an authorized member. For admission each prospective member must have the requisite qualifications.

The Club holds monthly meetings (first Monday of each month) for members only and quarterly socials for members, spouses, and children.

The Evans County Wildlife Club is a member of the Claxton-Evans County Chamber of Commerce and the Georgia Wildlife Federation.

A non-profit organization, the Wildlife Club annually donates to charities and organizations, including The American Cancer Society, the American Heart Association,

American Red Cross, The Evans County School System, Pinewood Christian Academy, Tattnall-Evans Training Center, Shriners, 4-H Club, sponsors the local Boy Scout Troop, and sponsors children to attend Camp Earthling through the Evans County Department of Family and Children's Services.

Each spring the Club sponsors a Fishing Rodeo for youngsters ages 5 through 16.

Throughout the year, the Club sponsors Georgia Hunter Education Programs with three Wildlife Cub members who are volunteer instructors.

$1,500.00, $1,000.00 and $500.00 college scholarships are awarded by the Club to Evans County students.

Club members donate their time each year during Rattlesnake Roundup Week to give informative talks to the students of the Evans County Elementary School System on rattlesnakes.

A Rattlesnake Roundup Queen is chosen each year to represent the Club and promote the Roundup in state-wide festivities and parades.

The Evans County Wildlife Club is sponsoring a "Teen dance" on Friday night this year at the Nedar Center.

The Annual Rattlesnake Roundup is by far our greatest accomplishment not only for the county, but for the country as well. Not only we the environment with the snake population, but we are able to contribute to medical research by providing venom to research labs.

The Club's accomplishments have been many. But without the support of the local businesses, city and county officials, and the citizens of Evans County, the Wildlife Club would not be the great success that it is today.

Rattlesnake Roundup Magazine—1995

AFTERWARD

At the very moment that David Wiggins was bitten by the Eastern Diamond Back Rattlesnake so many years ago, neither he nor perhaps no one else could have ever dreamed what the outcome would become.

Every year during the second weekend in March, thousands upon thousands of people both young and old, come from near and far to what was once called The Rattlesnake Roundup. Parades have been marched in. Children, wide-eyed and wondering and waiting anxiously as the clowns pass by. Young girls giggle as a kiss is planted upon their cheek by one of the clowns passing by.

Beauty pageant queens have been chosen and hundreds of snakes have been milked while being put on exhibition all the while spectators have watched.

Veterans show their pride by passing out little American flags to outreached hands ready to wait in admiral response.

The Wildlife Festival, as it is now known as drawn hundreds of thousands of people over the years. The legacy of the little boy from Claxton, Georgia, bitten all those many years ago, has surpassed anything anyone could have possibly ever imagined. He was indeed, chosen to rattle.

ACKNOWLEDGMENTS

Barnard, Keith; Cameron, Deana; Rountree, Sarah; Clifton, Preston; Deloach, Jessie; Durrence, Donna; Dyson Christy, Harper, Cathy; Harper, Lois; Hearn, Bill; Hodges, Frances; Miller, Angie; NeSmith, Mellie; Odom, Billy; Roberts, Gena; Sutton, Kathryn; Todd, Pam; Threatte, Greg; Tootle, Michelle; Wiggins, Cindy; Wiggins, David; Wiggins, Jeffrey; Wiggins, Jerry Williams, Pat;

Evans County Wildlife Festival

The Claxton Enterprise

www.ingramcontent.com/pod-product-compliance
Lightning Source LLC
Chambersburg PA
CBHW032029290526
45786CB00011B/1185